How to Start a Successful Career in Social Media for Beginners

A Step-by-Step Guide to Building a Thriving Social Media Presence and Landing Your Dream Job

The Fix-It Guy

Copyright © The Fix-It Guy

Table of Contents

Introduction

Are you tired of scrolling aimlessly through your social media feeds, wondering if there's more to life than memes, cat videos, and endless food photos? Well, guess what? There is!

Hello there, fellow internet dweller, and welcome to a journey that might just change your life. If you've ever dreamed of turning your love for social media into a thriving career, you're in the right place. We get it. The allure of Instagram filters and witty tweets can be oh-so-tempting. But what if I told you that behind the screens and hashtags lies a world of opportunities waiting for you?

Picture this: You, yes YOU, creating compelling content that not only goes viral but also pays your bills. Imagine landing your dream job in social media, whether it's managing a brand's online presence, becoming a sought-after influencer, or even pioneering the next big TikTok trend.

This book, "How to Start a Successful Career in Social Media for Beginners," isn't your typical snooze-worthy guide. We won't bore you with a dissertation on social media algorithms or confuse you with jargon that only tech wizards understand. Nope, we're here to break it down in plain, relatable language.

We'll guide you, step by step, through the exhilarating and, at times, bewildering world of social media. We're talking about finding your unique voice in a sea of status updates, making your pictures pop, connecting with an audience that can't get enough of your content, and even turning those likes and shares into a paycheck.

Are you ready to transform your scrolling habits into a well-paid, exciting career that puts you in control? This book is your golden ticket to the glittering world of social media success, and we're thrilled to have you on board. So, fasten your seatbelt (or should we say social belt?) and get ready for an adventure that's about to change the game. The journey begins now!

Chapter 1

Getting Started in Social Media

Defining Your Goals and Interests

In the digital realm of social media, where hashtags and trending topics reign supreme, it's easy to get lost in the vast sea of platforms and posts. But fear not! This chapter is your compass, helping you navigate the exciting world of social media with purpose and clarity.

Defining Your Goals and Interests
"Setting sail without a destination is like tweeting without a purpose."

At the core of your social media journey lies a fundamental question: Why are you here? Are you looking to boost your personal brand, share your creative talents, promote a cause, or perhaps establish a business empire? Defining your goals is the crucial first step toward a successful social media presence.

Why Defining Goals Matters:

1. Focus: Clear goals help you concentrate your efforts on what truly matters to you. Whether it's gaining followers, driving website traffic, or increasing sales, having a specific objective gives your social media activities direction.

2. Measurement: Goals provide measurable outcomes. By defining your goals, you can track your progress and adjust your strategies accordingly. Are you gaining followers? Are your posts engaging your audience? Setting benchmarks allows you to assess your success.

3. Authenticity: Knowing your goals keeps your content authentic. Your audience can sense sincerity. When your posts align with your objectives, your passion shines through, attracting like-minded individuals who resonate with your message.

Discovering Your Interests:
"Passion is the fuel that powers the social media engine."

Identifying your interests goes hand in hand with defining your goals. Your interests fuel your creativity, making your content unique and engaging. Whether you're passionate about travel, food, technology, fashion, or any other niche, your enthusiasm will draw in an audience that shares your interests.

How to Discover Your Interests:

1.   Soul-Searching: Reflect on your hobbies, experiences, and the topics that excite you. What could you talk about for hours without getting bored? Your genuine enthusiasm will resonate with others.

2. Market Research: Explore existing social media accounts and blogs within your areas of interest. Analyze what content works well and what doesn't. This research can inspire your own unique approach and style.

3. Experimentation: Don't be afraid to try different topics and content styles. Your interests might evolve as you explore. Experimentation allows you to find your voice and discover what truly captivates your audience.

Choosing the Right Social Media Platforms

"Different strokes for different folks, and different platforms for different voices."

Not all social media platforms are created equal. Each one has its unique vibe, audience, and purpose. To make a splash in the social media universe, you need to choose the right platforms that align with your goals and interests.

Factors to Consider When Choosing Social Media Platforms:

1. Audience: Different platforms attract different demographics. For instance, Instagram is popular among younger users and visual content enthusiasts, while LinkedIn caters to professionals and businesses. Know your target audience and pick platforms where they hang out.

2. Content-Type: Consider the type of content you plan to create. If you're into short, snappy videos, platforms like TikTok might be your playground. If you prefer sharing insightful articles, platforms like Medium or LinkedIn could be your go-to spaces.

3. Features: Each platform offers unique features. Twitter is known for its concise microblogging, Instagram for its visually appealing posts, and YouTube for video content. Explore the features and choose platforms that align with your content style and creativity.

4. Time Commitment: Managing multiple social media accounts can be time-consuming. Evaluate how much time you can realistically dedicate to social media. It's better to excel on a couple of platforms than to spread yourself thin across many.

Setting Up Your Profiles Effectively

"Your profile is your digital first impression; make it count!"

Now that you've chosen your platforms, it's time to create profiles that dazzle. Your social media profiles are your online identity, so it's essential to optimize them effectively.

Tips for Setting Up Effective Social Media Profiles:

1. Consistent Branding: Use consistent profile pictures, usernames, and bios across all platforms. This consistency builds brand recognition and trust among your audience.

2. Compelling Bio: Write a captivating and concise bio that conveys who you are and what you do. Use keywords related to your interests or industry to enhance discoverability.

3. Engaging Content: Populate your profile with engaging content right from the start. Upload eye-catching photos, videos, or posts that represent your style and interests. A visually appealing profile is more likely to attract followers.

4. Contact Information: Provide contact details or links to your website/portfolio if applicable. Make it easy for people to get in touch with you or explore your work further.

5. Privacy Settings: Adjust privacy settings based on your preferences. Some content might be suitable for public viewing, while others are best kept private or shared with specific groups.

Remember, your social media profiles are dynamic. Regularly update them with fresh content, engage with your audience, and adapt your profile information as your interests and goals evolve. By choosing the right platforms and setting up your profiles effectively, you're laying the groundwork for a strong social media presence that captures attention and leaves a lasting impression. Now, go ahead and let your digital personality shine!

Chapter 2

Building a Strong Personal Brand

Crafting Your Unique Selling Proposition (USP)

"In a world full of noise, your brand is your voice, your story, your essence - make it unforgettable."

In the vast digital landscape of social media, your brand is your most powerful asset. It's what sets you apart, making you memorable, relatable, and ultimately, successful. In this chapter, we delve into the art of crafting a Unique Selling Proposition (USP) that not only defines your brand but also captivates your audience.

"Your USP is the secret sauce that makes your brand sizzle."

Your Unique Selling Proposition is the distinctive blend of qualities, skills, and personality traits that make you unique. It's the essence of what you offer to the world, and it's the magnetic force that draws people to you. Defining your USP is like uncovering the hidden gem within you and showcasing it to the world.

How to Craft an Irresistible USP:

1. Self-Reflection: Reflect on your strengths, passions, and values. What are you genuinely passionate about? What skills do you excel at? What values drive your decisions? Your USP should align with your authentic self.

2. Identify Your Unique Qualities: What makes you different from others in your field? It could be a unique perspective, a specialized skill, or a distinctive personality trait. Identify what sets you apart and emphasize these qualities in your branding.

3. Address Pain Points: Understand the challenges your audience faces and how your skills or expertise can address these pain points. Your USP should provide a solution or fulfill a need for your audience, making you indispensable to them.

4. Be Authentic: Authenticity is the cornerstone of a compelling USP. Don't try to be someone you're not. Embrace your quirks, passions, and imperfections.

Authenticity builds trust and genuine connections with your audience.

5. Craft a Clear Message: Condense your USP into a clear, concise message that instantly communicates who you are and what you offer. Your message should be easy to understand and resonate emotionally with your audience.

Why Your USP Matters:

1. Differentiation: In a crowded social media landscape, your USP sets you apart from competitors. It gives people a reason to choose you over others in your niche.

2. Attracts the Right Audience: A well-defined USP attracts an audience that appreciates your unique qualities and what you have to offer. It filters out those who might not resonate with your brand, ensuring you connect with the right people.

3. Consistency: Your USP provides a consistent foundation for your content, visuals, and messaging across social media platforms. Consistency strengthens your brand identity and makes you instantly recognizable.

By crafting a compelling Unique Selling Proposition, you're not just building a personal brand; you're creating a magnetic force that draws people who resonate with your essence. Your USP is the heart of your social media presence, shaping your content, interactions, and relationships. Embrace your uniqueness, and let your brand shine brightly in the digital world. Your authentic voice is your superpower, use it to leave a lasting impact!

Creating a Consistent Brand Identity

"Consistency breeds familiarity, and familiarity builds trust."

In the noisy and ever-changing landscape of social media, a consistent brand identity is your beacon of recognition. It's what makes your audience recognize your content at a glance and builds trust in your authenticity. In this section, we'll explore the importance of a consistent brand identity and how to develop it effectively.

Why Consistent Brand Identity Matters:

1. Recognition: A consistent visual style, color scheme, and logo help people instantly recognize your content amidst the sea of posts. Consistency breeds familiarity, making your brand memorable.

2. Professionalism: A cohesive and polished brand identity reflects professionalism. It shows that you take your online presence seriously, which can positively influence how your audience perceives you.

3. Trust: When your audience knows what to expect from your brand, be it in visuals, content, or messaging, it creates a sense of trust. Consistency reassures your audience, building a strong bond between you and your followers.

How to Create a Consistent Brand Identity:

1. Define Your Visual Elements: Choose a specific color palette, typography, and imagery style that aligns with your brand personality. Use these elements consistently across all your social media platforms, ensuring a cohesive look and feel.

2. Craft a Memorable Logo: If applicable, design a logo that represents your brand essence. Your logo should be versatile and easily recognizable, whether it's displayed as a profile picture or in your content.

3. Maintain Consistent Tone: Your written content, captions, and messaging should carry a consistent tone. Whether it's friendly, professional, witty, or informative, maintain the same tone across all interactions to reinforce your brand's personality.

Developing Your Brand Voice and Tone
"Your words are your brand's melody, choose them wisely, and your audience will sing along."

Your brand voice and tone are the linguistic aspects of your identity. They encompass how you communicate with your audience, the language you use, and the emotions you evoke. Developing a distinct and relatable brand voice is key to creating a memorable social media presence.

Tips for Developing Your Brand Voice and Tone:

1. Know Your Audience: Understand the demographics, preferences, and communication styles of your target audience. Tailor your voice to resonate with them, using language and references they can relate to.

2. Stay Authentic: Your brand voice should reflect your personality and values. Whether you're humorous, inspirational, or educational, be true to who you are. Authenticity builds genuine connections with your audience.

3. Be Consistent Across Platforms: Maintain a consistent tone across all social media platforms. Whether you're posting a witty tweet, a heartfelt Instagram caption, or a professional LinkedIn update, ensure your tone remains coherent.

4. Adapt to Context: While your voice should remain consistent, adapt your tone to suit the context of the content. A celebratory tone might be suitable for achievements, while a compassionate tone works well for empathy-driven messages.

Chapter 3

Content Creation and Curation

Understanding Content Types (Text, Images, Videos)

"In the world of social media, content is king. Understanding the different content types is your ticket to the kingdom."

In the dynamic realm of social media, content comes in various forms, each with its unique appeal and impact. Whether you're crafting a compelling story, sharing captivating visuals, or producing engaging videos, understanding the nuances of different content types is essential. In this section, we'll explore the power of text, images, and videos, helping you leverage each medium to its fullest potential.

Text: Crafting Stories and Messages

"Words have the power to inspire, inform, and ignite emotions. Use them wisely."

Text-based content remains a cornerstone of social media. From witty tweets to in-depth blog posts, words can convey your thoughts, tell stories, and connect with your audience on a profound level.

How to Create Engaging Text Content:

1. Clarity and Conciseness: Be clear and concise in your messaging. Capture attention quickly and deliver your message succinctly. Short paragraphs and bullet points enhance readability.

2. Emotion and Storytelling: Infuse emotion into your text. Stories create connections and evoke empathy. Whether it's a personal anecdote or a customer testimonial, stories humanize your brand.

3. Call to Action (CTA): Encourage your audience to take action. Whether it's liking a post, sharing content, or visiting your website, include a clear and compelling CTA to guide your audience's next steps.

Images: Painting Pictures with Pixels
"A picture is worth a thousand words. An engaging image can speak volumes to your audience."

Visual content, especially images, has the power to captivate, inspire, and convey complex messages at a glance. Stunning visuals can evoke emotions, tell stories, and create a lasting impact.

Tips for Creating Visually Appealing Images:

1. High Quality: Use high-resolution images to maintain clarity and professionalism. Blurry or pixelated images can diminish the visual appeal of your content.

2. Relevance: Ensure that your images are relevant to your content and brand. Consistency in visual style enhances brand recognition.

3. Creativity: Experiment with graphic design tools, filters, and effects to add creativity to your visuals. Eye-catching designs and unique aesthetics grab attention.

Videos: Bringing Stories to Life
"Video is the most powerful way to humanize your brand, to bring your stories to life, and make your message memorable."

Video content is king in the social media world. From short clips to longer narratives, videos offer a dynamic way to engage your audience, share experiences, and convey complex information effectively.

Creating Compelling Videos:

1. Storyboarding: Plan your video content with a clear storyline. Structure your video with a beginning, middle, and end. A well-planned narrative keeps viewers engaged.

2. Visual Appeal: Pay attention to visual quality, lighting, and composition. Crisp visuals and smooth transitions enhance the overall viewing experience.

3. Duration: Consider the platform and audience preferences when determining video length. Short videos are ideal for quick engagement, while longer videos allow for in-depth storytelling.

Understanding the nuances of text, images, and videos empowers you to tailor your content to different platforms and audience preferences. Whether you're weaving a compelling story with words, painting vivid pictures with images, or bringing narratives to life through videos, each content type offers a unique opportunity to connect with your audience.

Mastering Content Creation Tools

"In the digital age, your creativity is amplified by the tools you master. Equip yourself with the right tools, and your content will soar."

Creating eye-catching and professional content doesn't have to be daunting. With a plethora of content creation tools available, you can unleash your creativity and bring your ideas to life. Whether you're a graphic designer, photographer, or video enthusiast, mastering the right tools can significantly enhance your content creation skills.

Types of Content Creation Tools:

1. Graphic Design Tools: Tools like Adobe Photoshop, Canva, and PicMonkey empower you to design stunning visuals, social media posts, and promotional materials. These platforms offer pre-made templates and easy-to-use interfaces, making graphic design accessible to everyone.

2. Video Editing Software: Software like Adobe Premiere Pro, Final Cut Pro, and iMovie allows you to edit videos, add special effects, and create engaging video content. With the rise of mobile video editing apps, such as InShot and Kinemaster, you can edit videos directly from your smartphone.

3. Photography Apps: Smartphone apps like Adobe Lightroom, VSCO, and Snapseed provide powerful editing tools for enhancing your photos. From adjusting lighting and colors to applying filters, these apps enable you to transform ordinary photos into visually appealing masterpieces.

4. Content Planning and Scheduling Tools: Platforms like Buffer, Hootsuite, and Later allow you to plan and schedule your social media posts in advance. These tools offer features like content calendars, post-scheduling, and analytics, helping you maintain a consistent online presence.

Curating Engaging and Relevant Content

"Curating content is an art. It's about finding the right blend of information, entertainment, and inspiration that resonates with your audience."

While creating original content is essential, curating content from various sources adds value to your social media presence. Curated content not only diversifies your feed but also positions you as a knowledgeable and well-informed authority in your niche.

Tips for Curating Engaging and Relevant Content:

1. Know Your Audience: Understand the preferences and interests of your audience. Curate content that aligns with their needs, challenges, and aspirations. Tailor your curated content to cater to your specific target demographic.

2. Quality over Quantity: Focus on quality curated content rather than overwhelming your audience with a flood of posts. Select content that is informative, entertaining, and thought-provoking. High-quality curated content enhances your credibility and keeps your audience engaged.

3. Diversify Content Sources: Curate content from a variety of sources, including reputable websites, industry influencers, and thought leaders. Diversifying your sources ensures a well-rounded perspective and prevents your content from becoming one-dimensional.

4. Add Value: When sharing curated content, add your insights, comments, or a compelling introduction. Explain why you find the content valuable or how it relates to current trends or events. Adding value enhances the relevance and context of the curated content.

5. Stay Consistent: Maintain a consistent schedule for curated content. Whether it's a weekly roundup or a daily share, consistency helps your audience anticipate and engage with your curated content regularly.

By mastering content creation tools and curating engaging and relevant content, you enrich your social media presence, attract a broader audience, and establish yourself as an authority in your field. Remember, creativity knows no bounds in the digital age, and with the right tools and curated content strategy, your social media platforms can become vibrant showcases of your expertise and passion. So, dive in, explore the tools, and curate content that captivates and informs your audience!

Chapter 5

Growing Your Social Media Presence

Building an Authentic Follower Base

"In the world of social media, genuine connections matter more than numbers. Focus on building relationships, and your followers will follow."

Congratulations! You've defined your goals, honed your brand, and created compelling content. Now comes the exciting part: growing your social media presence. In this chapter, we'll explore the art of building an authentic follower base that not only increases your numbers but also cultivates meaningful connections with your audience.

Building an Authentic Follower Base

"Authenticity is magnetic. Be real, be you, and watch your follower base grow organically."

While it might be tempting to chase after high follower counts, the true essence of social media success lies in the authenticity of your connections. Authentic followers are not just numbers on your profile; they are real people who engage with your content, share your passion, and believe in your message.

Strategies for Building an Authentic Follower Base:

1. Engage Authentically: Respond to comments, messages, and interactions genuinely. Engaging with your audience shows that you value their presence and opinions. Acknowledge their contributions, whether it's a simple like or a heartfelt reply.

2. Share Personal Stories: Vulnerability builds connections. Share personal anecdotes, challenges you've overcome, or behind-the-scenes glimpses of your life. Authentic storytelling humanizes your brand, making you relatable and approachable.

3. Showcase Your Expertise: Share your knowledge and expertise in your niche. Offer valuable tips, advice, and insights that demonstrate your authority. When people find value in your content, they are more likely to follow and engage with you.

4. Collaborate and Cross-Promote: Collaborate with influencers, peers, or brands within your niche. Cross-promotion introduces your profile to a wider audience who might resonate with your content. Collaboration fosters mutual respect and can lead to organic follower growth.

5. Be Consistent: Consistency is key to building trust and credibility. Post regularly and maintain a consistent posting schedule. When followers know when to expect your content, they are more likely to stay engaged and loyal.

6. Encourage User-Generated Content: Encourage your followers to create content related to your brand. Whether it's a challenge, hashtag campaign, or creative contest, user-generated content not only boosts engagement but also fosters a sense of community.

7. Authenticity Over Quantity: Focus on the quality of your connections rather than the quantity. Authentic followers are more likely to engage with your content, share it with others, and support your endeavors.

Remember, building an authentic follower base takes time and patience. It's not about overnight success but about nurturing genuine relationships that stand the test of time. Authenticity is magnetic; when you are true to yourself and your audience, you naturally attract followers who resonate with your message.

Increasing Engagement with Your Audience

"Engagement isn't a one-way street; it's a conversation. Listen, respond, and watch your community thrive."

Social media isn't just about broadcasting your message; it's about fostering meaningful connections and conversations with your audience. Increasing engagement is the key to building a vibrant online community. Engaged followers are more likely to interact with your content, share it with others, and become loyal advocates for your brand.

Strategies for Increasing Engagement:

1. Ask Questions: Encourage your audience to share their thoughts and opinions. Ask open-ended questions that invite discussions. Polls and surveys are excellent tools for gathering feedback and engaging your followers.

2. Respond Promptly: Acknowledge comments, messages, and mentions promptly. Responding promptly shows that you value your audience's input and encourages further interaction.

3. Host Live Sessions: Live videos create a sense of immediacy and allow real-time interaction with your audience. You can host Q&A sessions, tutorials, behind-the-scenes glimpses, or interviews, engaging directly with your viewers.

4. Run Contests and Giveaways: Contests and giveaways generate excitement and encourage participation. Whether it's a photo contest, caption competition, or prize giveaway, these events boost engagement and create buzz around your brand.

5. Share User-Generated Content: Showcase content created by your followers. This not only acknowledges their efforts but also strengthens the sense of community. User-generated content fosters a feeling of belonging and encourages others to participate.

6. Create Interactive Content: Utilize interactive features like polls, quizzes, and interactive stories. Interactive content encourages active engagement, allowing your audience to participate rather than just passively consume.

7. Express Gratitude: Show appreciation for your followers. Regularly express gratitude for their support and contributions. A simple thank-you message or shoutout can go a long way in building a positive relationship with your audience.

Utilizing Hashtags and Trends Effectively

"Hashtags and trends are the keys to unlocking a broader audience. Use them strategically, and watch your reach skyrocket."

Hashtags and trends are powerful tools to increase the visibility of your content and attract a wider audience. When used effectively, they can amplify your reach, connect you with like-minded individuals, and enhance your content's discoverability.

Tips for Utilizing Hashtags and Trends:

1. Research Relevant Hashtags: Identify popular and niche-specific hashtags related to your content and industry. Research trending hashtags on different platforms and incorporate them into your posts.

2. Create Branded Hashtags: Develop unique and memorable hashtags specific to your brand or campaigns. Branded hashtags encourage your followers to participate and create a sense of community around your brand.

3. Stay Current with Trends: Keep an eye on trending topics, events, and challenges within your niche. Joining relevant trends shows that you're in touch with the community and allows you to participate in conversations that are already capturing attention.

4. Be Creative: Don't hesitate to create your trends or challenges. Unique and creative ideas can catch on quickly, especially if they resonate with your audience's interests and passions.

5. Use Hashtags Sparingly: While hashtags are valuable, avoid overloading your posts with too many of them. Aim for a balance; use a mix of popular, niche, and branded hashtags to maximize reach without cluttering your content.

By actively engaging with your audience and utilizing hashtags and trends effectively, you're not only increasing your content's visibility but also nurturing a thriving online community. Social media is a two-way street; embrace the conversations, celebrate the interactions, and watch your engagement soar, creating a vibrant digital space where your audience feels heard, valued, and inspired. So, join the conversation, embrace the trends, and let your engagement strategies transform your social media presence into a dynamic and interactive hub!

Chapter 5

Social Media Strategy and Analytics

Developing a Social Media Strategy

"A well-crafted strategy and keen analysis are the twin engines that drive social media success. Plan thoughtfully, measure diligently, and watch your online presence soar."

In the bustling world of social media, having a well-defined strategy is your guiding star. It not only provides direction but also helps you make informed decisions based on data and insights. In this chapter, we'll explore the art of developing a robust social media strategy and understanding the power of analytics in refining your approach.

Developing a Social Media Strategy
"Strategy without tactics is the slowest route to victory. Tactics without strategy is the noise before defeat." – Sun Tzu

Creating a social media strategy is akin to planning a voyage. It involves setting clear objectives, identifying your target audience, choosing the right platforms, and crafting compelling content. A well-developed strategy aligns your efforts, ensuring that every post and interaction serves a purpose.

Steps to Develop an Effective Social Media Strategy:

1. Set Clear Goals: Define specific, measurable, achievable, relevant, and time-bound (SMART) goals for your social media presence. Whether it's increasing brand awareness, driving website traffic, or boosting engagement, clear objectives provide focus.

2. Know Your Audience: Understand your target audience's demographics, interests, and online behavior. Tailor your content and messaging to resonate with their preferences and motivations.

3. Choose the Right Platforms: Select social media platforms that align with your audience and goals. Different platforms cater to distinct demographics and content styles. Focus your efforts on platforms where your audience is most active.

4. Content Planning: Plan your content calendar thoughtfully. Balance promotional posts with educational, entertaining, and inspirational content. Consistency in content types and themes creates a cohesive brand identity.

5. Engagement Strategy: Outline how you'll engage with your audience. Determine response times, community management practices, and strategies for fostering conversations. Active engagement builds trust and loyalty.

6. Content Calendar: Create a content calendar outlining the topics, formats, and posting schedules. A content calendar ensures a consistent flow of content and helps you stay organized and proactive.

7. Monitor and Adjust: Regularly assess your strategy's performance. Monitor key metrics, analyze audience feedback, and adapt your approach based on insights. Flexibility and adaptability are essential in the ever-changing social media landscape.

Understanding Social Media Analytics

"Data is not just numbers; it's the story of your audience's interactions with your brand. Listen to the story, and you'll unlock the secrets to success."

Social media analytics provide invaluable insights into your audience's behavior, content performance, and overall impact. By understanding these metrics, you can refine your strategy, enhance engagement, and achieve your goals more effectively.

Key Social Media Metrics to Monitor:

1. Engagement Rate: Measure likes, comments, shares, and other interactions per post. A high engagement rate indicates that your content resonates with your audience.

2. Reach: Evaluate the number of unique users who see your content. Reach gives you an idea of your content's visibility and potential impact.

3. Click-Through Rate (CTR): CTR measures the percentage of users who click on a link in your post. It's crucial to assess the effectiveness of your calls to action.

4. Conversion Rate: Measure the percentage of users who complete a desired action, such as making a purchase or signing up for a newsletter. Conversion rate helps you assess the effectiveness of your social media campaigns.

5. Follower Growth: Track your follower count over time. Follower growth indicates your platform's overall popularity and the effectiveness of your engagement and content strategies.

6. Sentiment Analysis: Understand the sentiment behind user comments and interactions (positive, negative, or neutral). Sentiment analysis helps you gauge the audience's perception of your brand.

7. Referral Traffic: Monitor the traffic directed to your website from social media platforms. Analyzing referral traffic helps you assess the impact of your social media efforts on website visits and conversions.

By developing a well-crafted social media strategy and harnessing the power of analytics, you're not just navigating the digital landscape; you're thriving in it. A strategic approach, coupled with data-driven insights, empowers you to make informed decisions, strengthen audience connections, and achieve your social media objectives with precision.

Measuring Success: Key Metrics and Analytics Tools

"Success is not just about how far you've come; it's also about how smartly you've navigated the journey. Metrics and analytics are your compass, guiding you toward your goals."

Measuring the success of your social media efforts is paramount to understanding what works, what doesn't, and how to improve. Key metrics and analytics tools provide the insights necessary to make informed decisions and refine your strategy effectively.

Key Metrics to Measure Social Media Success:

1. Engagement Metrics: Assess likes, comments, shares, and clicks to understand how users interact with your content. High engagement signifies active audience participation and interest in your brand.

2. Reach and Impressions: Track the number of unique users who have seen your content (reach) and how many times your content was displayed (impressions). These metrics indicate the visibility and impact of your posts.

3. Click-Through Rate (CTR): CTR measures the percentage of users who click on a link or call to action in your content. It helps evaluate the effectiveness of your content in driving traffic to your website or landing pages.

4. Conversion Rate: Measure the percentage of users who complete a desired action, such as making a purchase or signing up for a newsletter. Conversion rate provides valuable insights into the effectiveness of your social media campaigns in driving tangible results.

5. Follower Growth: Monitor your follower count over time to assess the growth and popularity of your social media accounts. A steady increase in followers indicates a growing audience base.

6. Sentiment Analysis: Evaluate the sentiment behind user comments and interactions to gauge audience perception. Positive sentiment signifies a favorable response, while negative sentiment may indicate areas that need improvement.

Popular Analytics Tools:

1. Google Analytics: Offers detailed website analytics, including referral traffic from social media platforms, user behavior, and conversion tracking.

2. Facebook Insights: Provides in-depth analytics for Facebook pages, including engagement metrics, audience demographics, and post-performance.

3. Twitter Analytics: Offers insights into tweet engagement, follower growth, and audience demographics, helping you understand your Twitter audience better.

4. Instagram Insights: Provides data on post reach, impressions, engagement, and audience demographics, enabling you to optimize your Instagram strategy.

5. LinkedIn Analytics: Offers insights into post-performance, follower demographics, and engagement metrics, helping you assess your LinkedIn content's impact.

Adapting Your Strategy Based on Analytics

"Adaptability is the secret sauce of social media success. Listen to what the data tells you, pivot your strategy, and watch your results soar."

Analyzing the metrics and insights derived from your social media activities is not enough; adapting your strategy based on this data is the key to continuous improvement. Here's how you can adapt your strategy effectively:

1. Identify Patterns: Look for patterns and trends in your analytics data. Identify content types, posting times, and topics that consistently perform well. Likewise, identify areas where improvement is needed.

2. Analyze Audience Behavior: Understand how your audience interacts with your content. Identify the type of content they engage with the most and the platforms where they are most active. Tailor your strategy to cater to their preferences.

3. Experiment and Iterate: Use A/B testing and experimentation to test different content formats, posting schedules, and calls to action. Analyze the results and iterate your strategy based on what works best for your audience.

4. Stay Updated: Social media platforms frequently update their algorithms and features. Stay updated with the latest changes and adapt your strategy accordingly. New features can provide fresh opportunities for engagement and visibility.

5. Embrace Feedback: Listen to feedback from your audience. Whether it's comments, messages, or surveys, use this feedback to understand your audience's needs and preferences. Address concerns and adapt your content strategy to meet their expectations.

By measuring success through key metrics and utilizing analytics tools, you gain valuable insights into your social media performance. These insights empower you to adapt and refine your strategy, ensuring that you are always in sync with your audience's preferences and behaviors. Social media success is not a one-time achievement but an ongoing journey of adaptation, learning, and growth. Embrace the data, pivot your approach, and watch your social media presence thrive in the ever-evolving digital landscape.

Chapter 6

Collaboration and Networking

Collaborating with Influencers and Brands

"In the world of social media, collaboration is the bridge that connects creativity, influence, and opportunity. Partner wisely, and your potential becomes limitless."

Social media thrives on connections. Collaboration and networking are the lifeblood of a vibrant online presence. In this chapter, we'll explore the art of collaboration, focusing on partnering with influencers and brands to expand your reach, enhance your credibility, and create mutually beneficial relationships.

Collaborating with Influencers and Brands
"Influence is not about the number of followers, it's about the depth of connection. Collaborate with those who resonate with your audience and share your values."

Influencers and brands possess unique strengths and audiences. Partnering with them can amplify your message, introduce you to new followers, and create engaging content that resonates with a wider audience.

Here's how to navigate collaborations effectively:

1. Identify Compatible Partners: Choose influencers and brands whose values align with yours and whose audience overlaps with your target demographic. A compatible partnership ensures authenticity and resonates genuinely with your audience.

2. Craft a Compelling Pitch: When reaching out for collaboration, be clear about your intentions and the benefits of the partnership. Highlight what makes your collaboration unique and how it adds value to both parties.

3. Mutually Beneficial Collaboration: Ensure that the collaboration benefits both you and your partner. Whether it's cross-promotion, shared content creation, or joint events, find ways to create value for both parties involved.

4. Maintain Authenticity: Authenticity is key to a successful collaboration. Encourage influencers and brands to be genuine to their voice. Authentic content resonates deeply with audiences, fostering trust and credibility.

5. Be Clear with Expectations: Set clear expectations from the beginning. Outline the scope of the collaboration, deadlines, deliverables, and any financial or material agreements. Clear communication ensures a smooth and fruitful partnership.

6. Create Engaging Content: Collaborate on creating content that tells a story, showcases your products or services, and engages the audience. Interactive and creative content captures attention and leaves a lasting impression.

7. Promote and Acknowledge: Promote the collaborative content across your social media platforms. Acknowledge and appreciate your partners by tagging them, sharing their content, and expressing gratitude for the collaboration.

8. Evaluate and Learn: After the collaboration, assess its impact. Analyze metrics, gather feedback, and evaluate the success of the partnership. Learn from the experience to refine future collaborations and strategies.

Leveraging Social Media for Professional Networking

"In the digital age, your network is your net worth. Social media opens doors, but meaningful connections build bridges."

In the realm of professional networking, social media serves as a powerful tool, connecting professionals from diverse backgrounds, industries, and corners of the globe. It transcends geographical barriers, enabling you to build a rich tapestry of meaningful connections. Here's how you can leverage social media effectively for professional networking:

1. Optimize Your Profiles: Your social media profiles are your digital business cards. Ensure they are complete, professional, and reflective of your skills and expertise. Use a clear profile picture, write a compelling bio, and showcase your professional achievements.

2. Join Relevant Groups and Communities: Participate in industry-specific groups, forums, and communities on platforms like LinkedIn and Facebook. Engage in discussions, share insights, and connect with professionals who share your interests.

3. Share Valuable Content: Regularly share content related to your industry or profession. It could be articles, research papers, or your own thought leadership pieces. Sharing valuable content positions you as an expert and attracts like-minded professionals to your network.

4. Engage Thoughtfully: Engage in conversations thoughtfully and respectfully. Respond to comments, offer insights, and be open to diverse viewpoints. Engaging in a positive and constructive manner enhances your reputation within the professional community.

5. Utilize LinkedIn: LinkedIn is a treasure trove for professional networking. Connect with colleagues, peers, mentors, and professionals you admire. Personalize your connection requests, explaining why you wish to connect, to enhance your chances of acceptance.

6. Attend Virtual Events and Webinars: Participate in virtual industry events, webinars, and online workshops. These events offer excellent opportunities to learn, connect with experts, and engage with fellow attendees. Don't hesitate to reach out to speakers and attendees after the event to continue the conversation.

7. Request Informational Interviews: Don't be afraid to reach out to professionals you admire for informational interviews. Respect their time, come prepared with thoughtful questions, and express genuine interest in their experiences and insights.

Building Meaningful Connections in the Industry

"Networking is not about just connecting people. It's about connecting people with people, people with ideas, and people with opportunities."

Building meaningful connections goes beyond the surface level. It involves understanding others' perspectives, offering support, and fostering genuine relationships. Here's how you can nurture meaningful connections within your industry:

1. Be Genuine: Authenticity is the foundation of meaningful connections. Be yourself, share your experiences, and express genuine interest in others. Authenticity creates trust and fosters deeper connections.

2. Be a Supportive Listener: Actively listen when engaging with others. Show empathy, understand their challenges, and offer support and encouragement. Being a supportive listener builds trust and strengthens connections.

3. Offer Help and Value: Identify ways in which you can assist your connections. It could be sharing resources, offering advice, or connecting them with relevant professionals. Offering value without expecting immediate returns creates a lasting impression.

4. Follow Up: After initial interactions, follow up with your connections. Send a thank-you message, share relevant articles, or offer assistance based on your previous conversation. Regular follow-ups demonstrate your genuine interest in maintaining the connection.

5. Be Respectful of Time: Respect the time and boundaries of your connections. Understand that everyone has busy schedules. Be concise and respectful in your communications, appreciating their time and attention.

6. Celebrate Others' Achievements: Acknowledge and celebrate the achievements of your connections. Whether it's a new job, a promotion, or a successful project, showing genuine happiness for their accomplishments strengthens your relationship.

Building meaningful connections in the industry is a journey of mutual respect, shared experiences, and collaborative growth. By leveraging social media effectively and fostering genuine relationships, you can create a robust professional network that supports your career aspirations, opens doors to opportunities, and enriches your professional journey.

Chapter 7

Monetizing Your Social Media Presence

Exploring Different Revenue Streams (Ads, Affiliate Marketing, Products)

"Turning your passion into profit is an art. With the right strategies, your social media presence can be a lucrative platform for multiple streams of income."

In today's digital landscape, social media platforms offer abundant opportunities to turn your online presence into a source of income. This chapter explores the various avenues for monetizing your social media presence, from traditional advertising to more innovative methods like affiliate marketing and creating your products.

Exploring Different Revenue Streams

1. Advertisements and Sponsored Posts:
   Social media platforms often offer ad programs where you can create targeted ads to reach a specific audience. Sponsored posts, where brands pay you to promote their

products or services, are another lucrative option. Authenticity is crucial; choose collaborations that align with your brand and resonate with your audience.

2. Affiliate Marketing:

Affiliate marketing involves promoting products or services and earning a commission for every sale made through your referral link. Many companies offer affiliate programs, allowing you to earn a percentage of the sales you drive. Choose products relevant to your niche and audience for higher conversion rates.

3. Selling Products or Services:

If you have a unique skill, craft, or expertise, social media platforms can serve as an excellent marketplace for your products or services. Whether it's handmade crafts, digital products, online courses, or consulting services, your social media following can become your customer base.

4. Membership and Subscription Services:

Platforms like Patreon allow you to offer exclusive content or services to your followers in exchange for a monthly subscription fee. This model works well for creators, artists, writers, and other content producers who can offer valuable, premium content to their dedicated audience.

5. *Crowdfunding and Donations:*

Crowdfunding platforms like Kickstarter or platforms like Buy Me a Coffee allow your followers to support your creative endeavors directly. Whether you're funding a project, supporting a cause, or simply seeking contributions, your social media presence can help you reach potential backers.

6. *Selling Merchandise:*

Creating and selling branded merchandise, such as apparel, accessories, or merchandise related to your content, can be a profitable venture. Social media platforms provide an excellent avenue to showcase your products and connect with potential buyers.

7. *Online Events and Webinars:*

Host virtual events, workshops, or webinars on topics related to your expertise. Charge attendees a fee for participation or offer premium content to paying customers. Social media platforms can be used to promote, register, and engage with attendees before and after the event.

Key Strategies for Successful Monetization:

1. Know Your Audience: Understand your audience's needs, preferences, and pain points. Tailor your monetization strategies to cater to their interests and provide value.

2. Quality Over Quantity: Focus on creating high-quality, engaging content. Authenticity and value-driven content build trust and credibility, essential for successful monetization.

3. Transparency and Integrity: Be transparent with your audience about any sponsored content, affiliate relationships, or paid promotions. Maintain your integrity to retain your audience's trust.

4. Diversify Your Income Streams: Relying on a single source of income can be risky. Diversify your revenue streams to create a stable and sustainable income.

5. Engage and Interact: Actively engage with your audience. Respond to comments, messages, and feedback. Building a strong community fosters loyalty and enhances your monetization potential.

Monetizing your social media presence requires a combination of strategic planning, audience understanding, and creativity. By exploring diverse revenue streams, staying authentic, and delivering value, you can transform your social media platforms into profitable ventures.

Negotiating Brand Partnerships and Sponsorships

"Negotiating brand partnerships is an art of balancing value, integrity, and mutual benefit. Effective negotiation can pave the way for long-term, successful collaborations."

Brand partnerships and sponsorships are vital avenues for monetizing your social media presence. Negotiating these agreements requires careful consideration of your value, the brand's expectations, and the terms of collaboration. Here are some key strategies for negotiating brand partnerships and sponsorships:

1. Know Your Worth:

Understand your audience, engagement rates, and the value you bring to the table. Consider your reach, content quality, and the specific demographics you cater to. Having a clear understanding of your worth forms the foundation of successful negotiations.

2. Research the Brand:

Familiarize yourself with the brand's values, products, and target audience. Tailor your pitch to demonstrate how your audience aligns with the brand's goals. Showing a genuine interest in the brand's mission can make your proposal more compelling.

3. Be Clear About Deliverables:

Clearly define what the brand will receive in return for their investment. Outline the number of posts, types of content, platforms, and any additional promotional activities you'll undertake. Specificity helps manage expectations and avoids misunderstandings later on.

4. Negotiate Compensation:

Negotiate compensation that reflects the value you bring. This can include monetary payment, free products, affiliate commissions, or a combination. Be prepared to justify your rates based on your reach, engagement, and the potential impact of your collaboration.

5. Draft a Detailed Contract:

Once terms are agreed upon, draft a comprehensive contract outlining all aspects of the collaboration, including deliverables, payment terms, usage rights, timelines, and exclusivity clauses. Consult legal professionals if needed to ensure the contract is thorough and protective of your interests.

Legal and Ethical Considerations in Monetization

"Ethics and legality are the cornerstones of a sustainable online business. Upholding these principles safeguards your reputation and ensures long-term success."

When monetizing your social media presence, it's essential to adhere to legal regulations and ethical standards. Here are crucial legal and ethical considerations to keep in mind:

1. Disclosure and Transparency:

Disclose any sponsored content, affiliate links, or paid partnerships clearly to your audience. Transparency builds trust and ensures compliance with advertising regulations in many jurisdictions.

2. Copyright and Intellectual Property:

Respect copyright laws and intellectual property rights. Don't use others' content without permission, and ensure your content is protected. Watermark your original creations to deter unauthorized use.

3. Data Protection and Privacy:

Understand data protection laws such as GDPR (General Data Protection Regulation) and comply with them. Safeguard your audience's privacy, and be mindful of how you collect, store, and utilize their data.

4. Taxation and Reporting:

Report your earnings accurately and pay applicable taxes. Keep records of your income, expenses, and collaborations. Consult a tax professional to ensure compliance with tax regulations.

5. Endorsement Guidelines:

Familiarize yourself with social media platform guidelines and advertising standards. Adhere to guidelines related to sponsored content, promotions, and endorsements. Non-compliance can lead to penalties or account suspension.

6. Ethical Content Creation:

Create content that is respectful, inclusive, and free from harmful stereotypes or misinformation. Upholding ethical standards in your content ensures a positive impact on your audience and avoids controversies.

7. Protecting Brand Reputation:

Choose brand partnerships carefully. Ensure the brands you collaborate with align with your values and ethics. Protecting your reputation is as important as monetization; controversial or unethical partnerships can harm your brand in the long run.

Chapter 8

Job Hunting and Career Development

Crafting an Outstanding Social Media Resume and Portfolio

"In the digital age, your online presence is your resume. Craft it wisely, and open the doors to exciting career opportunities and professional growth."

In the competitive landscape of job hunting and career development, your social media presence plays a pivotal role. This chapter delves into the art of crafting an outstanding social media resume and portfolio, guiding you on how to showcase your skills, expertise, and achievements effectively.

1. Optimize Your Social Media Profiles:

Ensure your LinkedIn, Twitter, and other professional profiles are complete and up-to-date. Use a professional profile picture, write a compelling headline, and provide a comprehensive summary of your skills and experiences. Tailor your profiles to align with your career goals.

2. Showcase Your Expertise:

Highlight your expertise through posts, articles, or tweets related to your industry. Share your insights, participate in discussions, and demonstrate your knowledge. Regularly contribute valuable content to establish yourself as a thought leader in your field.

3. Create a Professional Website or Blog:

Develop a personal website or blog to showcase your portfolio, achievements, and professional journey. Include samples of your work, testimonials, and case studies to provide tangible evidence of your skills and accomplishments.

4. Visual Content and Multimedia Portfolio:

Incorporate visual elements into your portfolio, such as infographics, videos, or presentations. Visual content adds depth and engagement, allowing potential employers to experience your work in a more interactive way.

5. Quantify Your Achievements:

When describing your experiences, quantify your achievements whenever possible. Use numbers, percentages, or specific results to demonstrate the impact of your work. Quantifiable achievements provide tangible evidence of your contributions.

6. Collect Testimonials and Recommendations:

Request recommendations and testimonials from colleagues, supervisors, or clients. Authentic testimonials validate your skills and work ethic, adding credibility to your social media resume.

7. Highlight Skills and Certifications:

List your skills and certifications prominently. Include technical skills, soft skills, and any relevant certifications you've acquired. Skills and certifications demonstrate your qualifications and expertise in specific areas.

8. Engage in Online Courses and Webinars:

Participate in online courses, webinars, and workshops related to your industry. Display your certifications or course completions on your profiles. Continuous learning demonstrates your commitment to professional development.

9. Curate a Diverse Portfolio:

Showcase a variety of projects, campaigns, or initiatives you've been involved in. A diverse portfolio demonstrates your adaptability and versatility, showcasing your ability to handle different aspects of your field.

10. Regularly Update Your Portfolio:

Your social media resume and portfolio should be dynamic and ever-evolving. Regularly update your profiles with new achievements, projects, or skills you acquire. Keeping your portfolio current reflects your ongoing growth and expertise.

In the digital age, your online presence is a powerful asset in your job hunting and career development journey. By crafting an outstanding social media resume and portfolio, you not only showcase your skills and experiences but also position yourself as a valuable asset to potential employers. Invest time and effort into curating a compelling online presence, and watch as doors to exciting career opportunities open wide, leading you to a fulfilling and successful professional journey.

Navigating Job Boards and Networking Events

"Job boards and networking events are not just platforms; they are gateways to your next opportunity. Navigate them with strategy, confidence, and genuine connections to open doors to your dream job."

In the digital age, job boards and networking events are essential tools for job seekers. Navigating these platforms effectively can significantly enhance your chances of landing your ideal social media position.

1. Optimize Your Job Board Profile:
Create a compelling profile on job boards like LinkedIn, Indeed, or Glassdoor. Use keywords relevant to your skills and the social media positions you're interested in. Complete all sections, showcasing your experience, education, and achievements. A well-optimized profile increases your visibility to potential employers.

2. Set Job Alerts:
Utilize job alerts to receive notifications about new social media job postings. Tailor your job alert settings to receive updates specific to your desired role, location, and industry. Being among the first applicants can give you a competitive advantage.

3. Actively Network on LinkedIn:

LinkedIn is a powerful platform for professional networking. Connect with professionals in your industry, join relevant groups, and participate in discussions. Engaging with industry peers and potential employers can lead to valuable connections and job opportunities.

4. Research and Prepare for Networking Events:

Before attending networking events, research the participating companies and individuals. Familiarize yourself with their work, recent achievements, and industry trends. Being well-informed demonstrates your genuine interest and can lead to meaningful conversations.

5. Prepare Your Elevator Pitch:

Craft a concise and engaging elevator pitch that introduces yourself, your skills, and your career goals. Your elevator pitch should be memorable and highlight your unique qualities. Practice delivering it confidently to make a lasting impression at networking events.

Interview Tips and Tricks for Social Media Positions

"An interview is not just an evaluation; it's a conversation. Showcase your skills, enthusiasm, and cultural fit to leave a lasting impression."

Interviewing for social media positions requires a combination of digital expertise, creativity, and professionalism. Here are some tips and tricks to ace your social media job interviews:

1. Showcase Your Online Presence:

Your social media profiles are a testament to your skills. Ensure they are professional, well-curated, and reflect your expertise. Be prepared to discuss specific campaigns, projects, or content you've created or managed.

2. Demonstrate Your Content Creation Skills:

Prepare a portfolio showcasing your content creation abilities. Include samples of posts, graphics, videos, or social media campaigns you've worked on. Demonstrating your creativity visually can leave a strong impression.

3. Understand the Company's Social Media Presence:

Research the company's social media profiles, content strategy, and engagement tactics. Discuss specific aspects you admire or would improve. Showing that you've done your homework demonstrates your genuine interest in the position.

4. Discuss Campaign Strategies and Metrics:

Be ready to discuss successful social media campaigns you've executed or ideas for future campaigns. Talk about the strategies you implemented, the metrics you tracked, and the outcomes achieved. Data-driven results can impress potential employers.

5. Emphasize Community Management Skills:

Social media is not just about posting content; it's about engaging with the audience. Highlight your community management skills, including how you respond to comments, handle feedback, and foster positive interactions with followers.

6. Address Challenges and Learning Experiences:

Be prepared to discuss challenges you've faced in social media management and how you resolved them. Emphasize your ability to adapt, learn from mistakes, and continuously improve your strategies.

7. Ask Thoughtful Questions:

Prepare insightful questions to ask the interviewer. Inquire about the company's social media goals, challenges they face, or the team's collaborative process. Thoughtful questions demonstrate your genuine interest in the role and the company.

8. Follow-Up After the Interview:

Send a thank-you email after the interview, expressing your gratitude for the opportunity to discuss the position. Use this chance to reiterate your enthusiasm for the role and briefly mention a key point from the interview discussion. A follow-up message showcases your professionalism and eagerness for the position.

By navigating job boards and networking events strategically and acing your social media job interviews, you position yourself as a strong contender for coveted positions in the digital marketing world. Remember, your unique skills, passion, and ability to showcase your expertise both online and in person are your most powerful assets. With confidence, preparation, and a genuine approach, you can navigate the job market successfully and land the social media position of your dreams.

With confidence, preparation, and a genuine approach, you can navigate the job market successfully and land the social media position of your dreams.

Chapter 9

Staying Relevant and Adapting to Trends

Keeping Up with Social Media Trends and Changes

"In the ever-evolving landscape of social media, adaptability is the key to relevance. Stay ahead of the curve, embrace change, and transform challenges into opportunities."

Social media is dynamic, with trends and platforms constantly evolving. To maintain a successful career and thriving online presence, it's essential to stay relevant and adapt to the ever-changing social media landscape. This chapter explores strategies for keeping up with social media trends and changes, ensuring your strategies remain fresh, engaging, and effective.

1. Continuous Learning and Skill Development:

Invest in continuous learning. Enroll in online courses, attend webinars, and read industry blogs and publications to stay updated with the latest social media trends, tools, and best practices. Acquiring new skills enhances your expertise and adaptability.

2. Follow Thought Leaders and Influencers:

Follow industry thought leaders, influencers, and experts on social media platforms. Their insights, analyses, and predictions can provide valuable information about emerging trends and changes. Engage with their content to stay informed and inspired.

3. Participate in Online Communities:

Join social media and digital marketing communities on platforms like LinkedIn, Facebook, or Reddit. Engage in discussions, share your experiences, and learn from others. These communities serve as valuable knowledge-sharing platforms where professionals exchange insights and trends.

4. Experiment with Emerging Platforms:

Stay curious and explore emerging social media platforms. Early adoption can provide a competitive advantage. Experiment with new features, content formats, and engagement strategies. Being an early adopter allows you to master the platform before it becomes mainstream.

5. Monitor Social Media Updates and Announcements:

Social media platforms frequently update their algorithms, features, and policies. Stay informed about these changes by following official announcements and updates from the platforms. Understanding platform changes helps you adapt your strategies accordingly.

6. Embrace Video and Live Streaming:

Video content and live streaming continue to dominate social media. Experiment with creating engaging videos, tutorials, and live streams. Platforms like YouTube, Instagram, Facebook, and TikTok offer diverse opportunities for video content creation.

7. Stay Data-Driven:

Use analytics tools to track the performance of your social media campaigns. Analyze engagement metrics, audience behavior, and content effectiveness. Data-driven insights provide valuable feedback, allowing you to optimize your strategies based on what works best for your audience.

8. Engage with Your Audience:

Actively engage with your audience. Respond to comments, conduct polls, and ask for feedback. Understanding your audience's preferences and interests firsthand helps you tailor your content to meet their expectations and stay relevant.

9. Collaborate and Network:

Collaborate with fellow professionals and influencers. Networking opens doors to diverse perspectives and insights. Collaborative projects can introduce you to new audiences and provide fresh ideas, keeping your content and strategies innovative.

10. Adapt to Cultural and Social Changes:

Social and cultural trends impact social media content. Stay aware of societal changes, global events, and cultural shifts. Adapting your content to resonate with current events and cultural nuances demonstrates your relevance and awareness.

In the fast-paced world of social media, staying relevant is not just about following trends; it's about understanding your audience, experimenting with new ideas, and adapting your strategies based on real-time data and feedback. Embrace change with enthusiasm, view challenges as opportunities to learn and grow, and let your adaptable mindset be your guide in navigating the ever-evolving landscape of social media. By staying relevant and adapting to trends, you not only maintain your online presence but also position yourself as a leader in the dynamic world of digital communication.

Continuous Learning: Courses, Workshops, and Certifications

"In the world of social media, knowledge is your superpower. Continuously upgrading your skills through education empowers you to stay ahead, innovate, and excel in your social media career."

Continuous learning is the cornerstone of a successful social media career. The digital landscape is constantly evolving, and staying updated with the latest trends, tools, and strategies is essential to remain competitive. Here are effective ways to engage in continuous learning:

1. Enroll in Online Courses: Platforms like Coursera, Udacity, and LinkedIn Learning offer a wide range of social media courses. From beginner to advanced levels, these courses cover topics such as social media marketing, content creation, analytics, and community management. Structured online courses provide in-depth knowledge and hands-on experience.

2. Attend Workshops and Webinars: Participate in workshops and webinars conducted by industry experts. These interactive sessions often focus on specific skills or emerging trends. Workshops offer a hands-on learning experience, allowing you to apply techniques in real-time. Webinars provide insights from professionals and can be a valuable source of inspiration.

3. Earn Industry-Recognized Certifications: Pursue certifications from reputable organizations like HubSpot, Hootsuite, or Google. Social media certifications validate your expertise and can enhance your credibility. These certifications cover various aspects of social media marketing, advertising, and analytics. Displaying certifications on your profile showcases your commitment to professional development.

4. Join Online Communities and Forums: Engage in social media and digital marketing communities. Platforms like Reddit, Facebook Groups, and industry-specific forums are excellent places to learn from peers, ask questions, and share experiences. Active participation in these communities exposes you to diverse perspectives and practical insights.

5. Participate in Online Challenges: Join social media challenges and campaigns related to your niche. Challenges encourage creativity and provide opportunities to learn from others. Engaging in challenges hones your skills, boosts your confidence, and expands your network within the social media community.

Future Predictions for Social Media Careers

"The future of social media careers is not just digital; it's dynamic. Embrace emerging technologies, adapt to changing platforms, and cultivate a mindset of innovation to thrive in the evolving landscape."

The future of social media careers holds exciting possibilities driven by technological advancements and changing user behaviors. Here are some predictions shaping the future of social media careers:

1. Augmented Reality (AR) and Virtual Reality (VR):

AR and VR technologies will revolutionize social media experiences. Social media platforms will integrate augmented and virtual reality features, offering immersive content and interactive marketing campaigns. Social media professionals skilled in AR and VR content creation will be in high demand.

2. Artificial Intelligence (AI) and Chatbots:

AI-driven tools and chatbots will play a significant role in customer service, content creation, and data analysis. Social media professionals will leverage AI to personalize user experiences, automate responses, and analyze vast amounts of data for strategic decision-making.

3. Video Continues to Dominate:

Video content will remain at the forefront of social media. Short-form videos, live streams, and interactive video formats will gain popularity. Social media specialists proficient in video production, editing, and storytelling will be sought after by brands and businesses.

4. Ephemeral Content and Stories:

Ephemeral content, such as Instagram Stories and Snapchat Snaps, will continue to engage users. Brands will leverage these formats for time-sensitive promotions, behind-the-scenes content, and interactive polls. Social media experts skilled in creating compelling ephemeral content will be in demand.

5. Ethical and Inclusive Marketing:

Ethical and inclusive marketing practices will gain prominence. Social media professionals will focus on creating diverse and inclusive content, championing social causes, and promoting sustainable practices. Brands will prioritize authenticity and social responsibility in their online presence.

6. Niche Communities and Micro-Influencers:

Niche communities and micro-influencers will gain traction. Brands will collaborate with influencers who have smaller but highly engaged audiences, fostering genuine connections with niche markets. Social media specialists adept at identifying and engaging with niche communities will excel.

7. Data Privacy and User Security:

Data privacy and user security will be paramount. Social media professionals will need to stay updated on regulations, user data protection laws, and platform policies. Understanding and implementing secure data practices will be essential to maintaining user trust.

Embracing continuous learning and being adaptable to emerging trends and technologies will be the foundation of a successful social media career. As the digital landscape evolves, social media professionals who proactively enhance their skills, stay ethical, and innovate their strategies will be well-positioned to navigate the future of social media careers with confidence and creativity.

Embracing continuous learning and being adaptable to emerging trends and technologies will be the foundation of a successful social media career

Conclusion

As we reach the final page of this journey, remember that your potential in the realm of social media is limitless. Armed with the knowledge, skills, and insights shared within these pages, you are not just equipped to start a successful career in social media, you're prepared to thrive.

Social media is not merely a digital landscape; it's a dynamic universe of endless possibilities. It's about crafting compelling narratives, building genuine connections, and embracing change with open arms. It's the art of leveraging technology to tell stories that resonate, create communities that thrive, and impact lives in meaningful ways.

Your journey in social media is not just about mastering algorithms or creating viral content; it's about understanding people, their aspirations, and their dreams. It's about being a catalyst for change, a source of inspiration, and a beacon of creativity.

So, as you step into the vibrant world of social media, be bold, be authentic, and be innovative. Embrace challenges as opportunities, learn from failures, and celebrate every success, big or small. Your story in social media is waiting to be written, and the canvas is yours.

With passion as your guide, knowledge as your foundation, and creativity as your fuel, go forth and craft your digital legacy. The world is listening, and your voice matters. Here's to your successful journey in social media and the incredible impact you're destined to make.

Wishing you endless creativity, boundless connections, and a future in social media that surpasses your wildest dreams.

Go write your story. The world is waiting.

Congratulations on your journey to success in social media. The adventure has just begun.

www.ingramcontent.com/pod-product-compliance
Lightning Source LLC
Chambersburg PA
CBHW062235290526
45794CB00006B/2293